United States General Accounting Office

GAO

Report to the Chairman, Subcommittee on Clean Air, Wetlands, Private Property, and Nuclear Safety, Committee on Environment and Public Works, U. S. Senate

April 2000

AIR POLLUTION

I0412762

Status of Implementation and Issues of the Clean Air Act Amendments of 1990

GAO

Accountability * Integrity * Reliability

GAO/RCED-00-72

Contents

Letter   3

Appendixes

Appendix I: Title I—National Ambient Air Quality Standards   22

Appendix II: Titles I and II—Mobile Sources   29

Appendix III: Title III—Hazardous Air Pollutants   34

Appendix IV: Title IV—Acid Deposition Control   38

Appendix V: Title V—Permit Program   41

Appendix VI: Title VI—Stratospheric Ozone Protection   48

Appendix VII: Selected Organizations Included in GAO's Review   51

Appendix VIII: Comments From the Environmental Protection Agency   53

Tables

Table 1: Status of Requirements Designed for National Ambient Air Quality Standards   23

Table 2: Long-Term Percent Changes in National Air Quality Concentration   24

Table 3: Status of Requirements Designed for Mobile Sources   30

Table 4: Status of Requirements Designed for Hazardous Air Pollutants   35

Table 5: Status of Requirements Designed for Acid Rain Deposition   39

Table 6: Status of Requirements Designed for the Permit Program   42

Table 7: Status of Requirements Designed for Stratospheric Ozone Protection   49

Figures

Figure 1: U.S. Population, Vehicle Miles Traveled, U.S. Gross Domestic Product, and Aggregate Pollution Emissions, 1970-97   8

Figure 2: Number of People Living in Counties With Air Quality Concentrations Above the Level of the National Ambient Air Quality Standards in 1997 (numbers in millions)   9

Figure 3: Status of Requirements   10

Contents

United States General Accounting Office
Washington, D.C. 20548

Resources, Community, and
Economic Development Division

B-284843

April 17, 2000

The Honorable James M. Inhofe
Chairman, Subcommittee on Clean Air, Wetlands,
Private Property, and Nuclear Safety
Committee on Environment and Public Works
United States Senate

Dear Mr. Chairman:

The Clean Air Act,[1] last reauthorized and amended by the Congress in 1990, provides for a number of related programs designed to protect health and control air pollution. The Clean Air Act Amendments of 1990 established new programs and made major changes in the ways that air pollution is controlled. The amendments require the Environmental Protection Agency (EPA) to take a number of actions—such as issuing new regulations and guidance documents, undertaking research studies, and preparing reports to the Congress—and specify a deadline for many of them. The majority of these requirements are found in the amendments' first six titles; EPA has identified 538 such requirements, 361 of which have a statutory deadline. Additionally, the amendments specify deadlines for states and local air pollution control agencies—who play a pivotal role in implementing the act—to respond to the rules promulgated by EPA.

---

[1]42 U.S.C. 7401-7626. Unless otherwise stated, in this report "the act" refers to the Clean Air Act as amended in 1990.

With reauthorization of the Clean Air Act impending, you asked us to provide information on the implementation of the first six titles of the 1990 Clean Air Act amendments.[2] Specifically, you asked us to (1) provide information on the status of EPA's implementation of the requirements established by the 1990 amendments and (2) obtain views from state governments, local programs, industries that are regulated under the act, and environmental advocacy groups (collectively referred to as stakeholders) on the issues that have either helped or hindered the implementation of the 1990 amendments.[3]

Results in Brief

As of February 2000, EPA had identified 538 requirements under the 1990 amendments' first six titles, of which 409 have been met. Of the requirements that have been met, 162 had no statutory deadlines, and the remaining 247 had statutory deadlines before the end of February 2000. EPA missed the statutory deadline for 198 of these 247 requirements with a deadline. Of the 129 requirements that the agency has not met, 6 had a statutory due date prior to February 2000, 108 have a statutory due date after February 2000, and 15 do not have a statutory due date. EPA will likely miss 62 of the 108 future statutory requirements, which are related to establishing new standards for hazardous air pollutants. EPA officials attributed the agency's missing of statutory deadlines to several reasons, including (1) an increased emphasis on stakeholders' review and involvement during the development of regulations, which added to the time needed to issue regulations; (2) the setting of priorities to manage the workload resulting from the 1990 amendments, which created a tremendous number of new responsibilities for EPA; and (3) complications associated with the startup and effective implementation of new programs, including technical, policy, or legal issues that were not fully anticipated in 1990.

Stakeholders provided a variety of views on the issues that have helped or hindered the implementation of the six titles. The following were the most commonly cited issues:

---

[2]This report does not address the implementation of requirements established prior to the 1990 amendments.

[3]A list of the specific stakeholders contacted for this report is in appendix VII.

- *The degree of flexibility allowed for states and regulated pollution sources to determine how they will achieve required air quality improvements.* A number of stakeholders expressed the view that flexibility in the act has helped implementation. For example, according to stakeholders, the emissions allowance-trading system–under which utilities that reduce their emissions below required levels can sell their allowances to other utilities to help them meet their requirements–established by the title dealing with acid rain is a good example of flexibility. This allows electric utilities to achieve required sulfur dioxide emissions reductions at a lower-than-expected cost. One of the challenges facing the Congress in considering the reauthorization of the Clean Air Act is determining the appropriate balance between traditional command and control approaches and more flexible approaches that allow states and local air pollution control agencies and other stakeholders to implement the most cost-effective strategies, while meeting national air quality goals.
- *The extent to which goals and requirements are clearly specified in the statute or regulations.* For example, stakeholders cited the specificity in the act's title dealing with stratospheric ozone depletion, which listed the affected chemicals and the dates for their eventual phase-out, as contributing to the successful implementation of that title.
- *The adequacy of resources at the state and local level to effectively implement and enforce the statute.* Stakeholders cited inadequate resources as an example of where the implementation of the 1990 amendments has been hindered.

Background

The Clean Air Act, enacted in 1963 and substantially overhauled in 1970, is a comprehensive federal law that regulates air emissions from stationary and mobile sources. This law authorizes EPA to, among other things, establish National Ambient Air Quality Standards (NAAQS) to protect public health and welfare. The goal of the 1970 amendments was to set and achieve the standards in every state by 1975. The setting of pollutant standards was coupled with directing the states to develop state implementation plans applicable to appropriate sources in the state. The Congress amended the statute again in 1977 primarily to set new goals or dates for attaining the standards, since many areas of the country had failed to meet the deadlines.

In large part, the 1990 amendments to the Clean Air Act were intended to meet unaddressed or insufficiently addressed problems. The major provisions of the amendments are contained in the first six titles. Each of these titles requires EPA to, among other things, promulgate regulations, publish final guidance for state air pollution control programs, and issue various research reports to the Congress. Most of the requirements involve promulgating regulations to implement the act. Once the regulations are promulgated, it is generally up to state and local air pollution control agencies to enforce their provisions, with oversight from EPA.

- Title I of the 1990 amendments establishes a more comprehensive approach for states to implement, maintain, and enforce the NAAQS.
- Title II contains provisions for controlling air pollution from motor vehicles, engines, and their fuel.
- Title III establishes new requirements to reduce the emissions of hazardous air pollutants (often called "air toxics").
- Title IV establishes the acid deposition control program to reduce the adverse effects of acid rain by reducing the annual emissions of pollutants that are precursors of acid rain.[4]
- Title V establishes a national permit program to ensure compliance with all applicable requirements of the act and to enhance EPA's and the states' ability to enforce the act. Title V requires the states to establish permit programs.
- Title VI establishes provisions to protect the stratospheric ozone layer.

Although the Clean Air Act is a federal law covering the entire country, the states are responsible for carrying out much of the statute. Under the law, EPA sets limits on how much of certain pollutants can be in the air anywhere in the United States. This ensures that all Americans have the same basic environmental protections. The 1990 amendments set deadlines for EPA, states, local governments, and businesses to reduce air pollution. These deadlines were designed to be more realistic than the deadlines in previous versions of the law.

---

[4]Acid deposition is caused mainly by coal that is burned in large electrical utility plants in the Midwest. When the coal is burned, large amounts of sulfur dioxide are released. It is then carried by winds toward the East Coast of the United States and Canada, where the acids become part of rain, snow, or fog in the area, or remain in gas or particle form and settle onto land as dry deposition. Falling to earth, acid rain can damage plant and animal life as well as lakes and streams.

According to EPA, by many measures, the quality of the nation's air has improved in recent years. Great strides have been made in combating urban air pollution, toxic air pollution, depletion of the stratospheric ozone layer, and acid rain. Specifically, ground-level ozone, particulate matter, and carbon monoxide emissions have been reduced; the emissions of toxic air pollution are expected to decrease by 1.5 million tons a year; production of the most harmful ozone depleting chemicals has ceased; sulfur dioxide emissions have been cut by more then 5 million tons from the 1980 level; and motor vehicles and fuels are far cleaner than in 1990 as a result of revised emissions standards. As shown in figure 1, while the United States enjoyed major increases in population, gross domestic product, and vehicle miles traveled, the aggregate emissions of the six criteria pollutants decreased by 31 percent from 1970 through 1997.[5]

---

[5]The six criteria pollutants are ozone, carbon monoxide, particulate matter, sulfur dioxide, nitrogen oxide, and lead. They are called criteria pollutants because the agency set permissible levels for them on the basis of "criteria" or information on the effects on public health or welfare that may be expected from the presence of such pollutants.

Figure 1: U.S. Population, Vehicle Miles Traveled, U.S. Gross Domestic Product, and Aggregate Pollution Emissions, 1970-97

Percentage

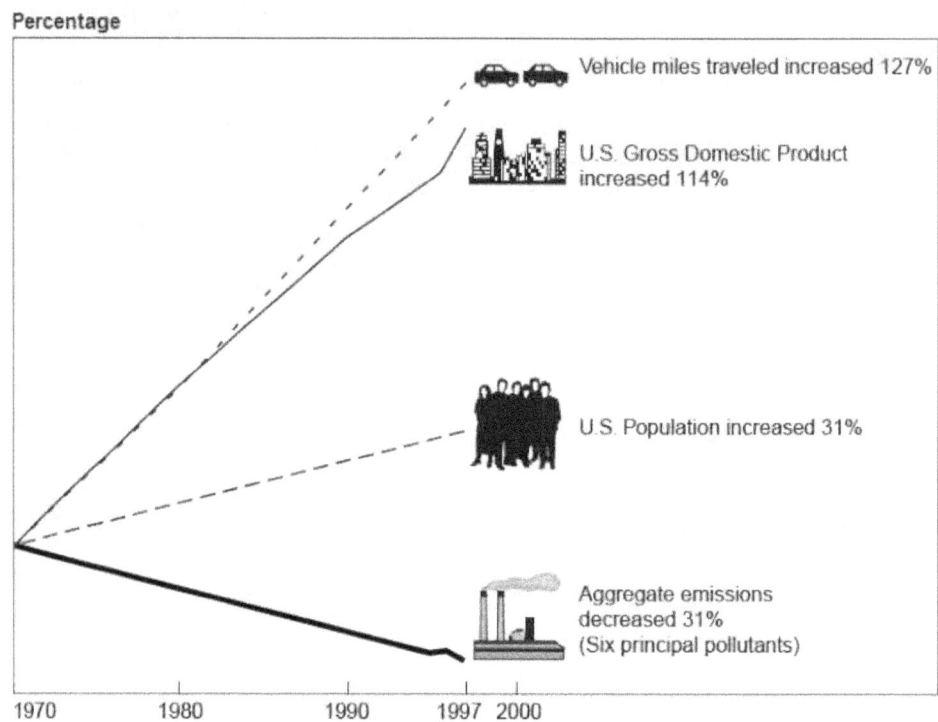

Source: EPA's *National Air Quality and Emissions Trends Report* (1997)

Although changes in the economy and other factors affect emissions trends, according to EPA, the emissions of air pollutants would be much higher without the Clean Air Act. EPA's Assistant Administrator for Air and Radiation has stated that the implementation of the Clean Air Act Amendments of 1990 has substantially cut air pollution over the past 9 years.[6] The stakeholders we interviewed—including environmental groups, industrial groups, and state and local governments—also agreed that the 1990 amendments have had a positive effect on the environment.

---

[6]Testimony of the Assistant Administrator, Office of Air and Radiation, Environmental Protection Agency, before the U. S. Senate, Committee on Environment and Public Works, Subcommittee on Clean Air, Wetlands, Private Property and Nuclear Safety (Oct. 14, 1999).

However, according to EPA's Assistant Administrator, the nation still has a long way to go to reach the agency's goal of clean air nationwide. For example, as shown in figure 2, in 1997, approximately 107 million people lived in counties with air pollutant concentrations that exceeded national ambient air quality standards.

Figure 2: Number of People Living in Counties With Air Quality Concentrations Above the Level of the National Ambient Air Quality Standards in 1997 (numbers in millions)

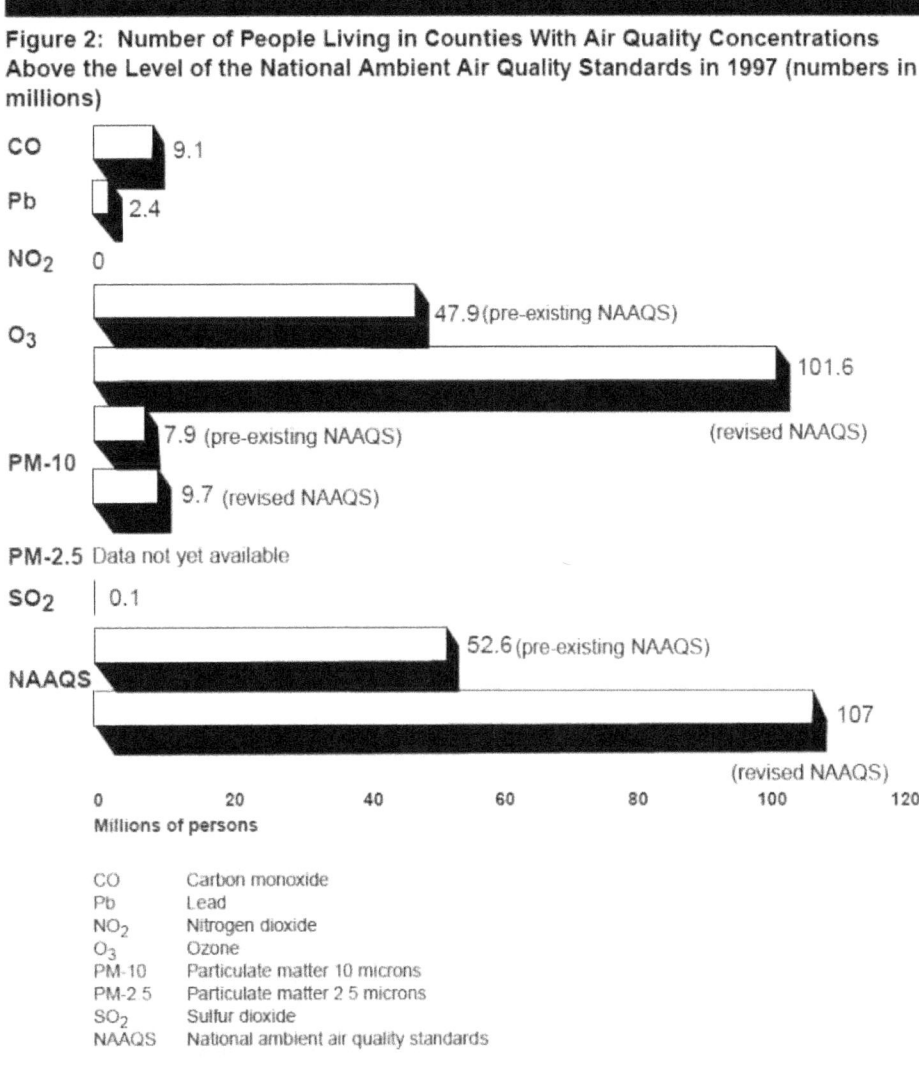

CO	Carbon monoxide
Pb	Lead
NO_2	Nitrogen dioxide
O_3	Ozone
PM-10	Particulate matter 10 microns
PM-2.5	Particulate matter 2.5 microns
SO_2	Sulfur dioxide
NAAQS	National ambient air quality standards

Source: EPA's *National Air Quality and Emissions Trends Report* (1997).

Status of EPA's Implementation of the Clean Air Act Amendments of 1990

As of February 2000, EPA had completed the majority of the actions required by the 1990 amendments. As shown in figure 3, the bulk of the future requirements relate to establishing new standards for hazardous air pollutants under title III, which will be completed in 2002, according to EPA officials' estimates. However, not all the requirements were met within the statutory deadline, and EPA officials indicated that additional requirements may be met after the specified statutory deadline, particularly those for the hazardous air pollutants. The status of implementing each of the amendments' six major titles is detailed in appendixes I through VI.

Figure 3: Status of Requirements

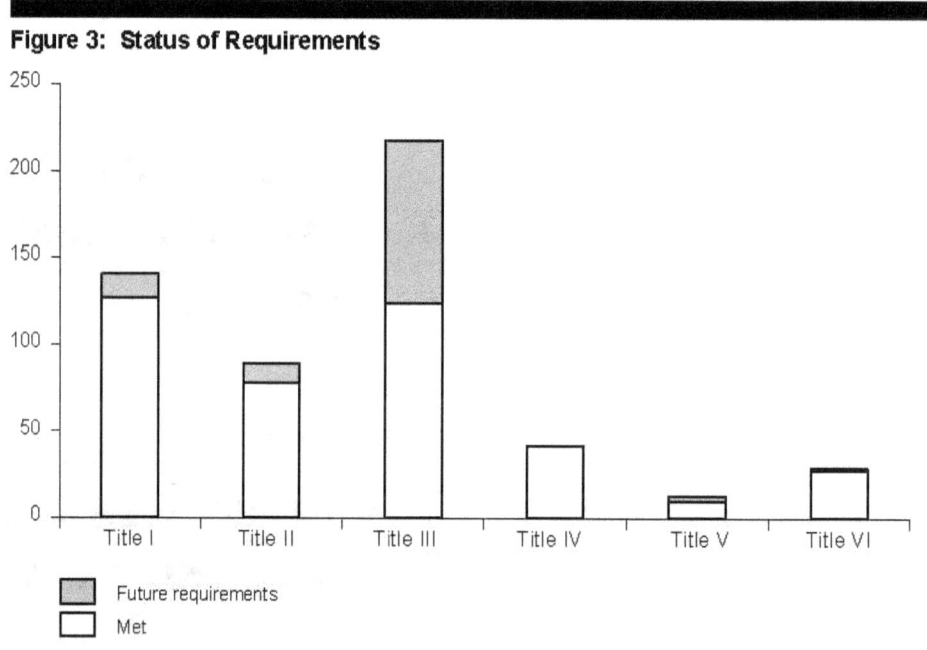

Note: There are six unmet requirements (one in title I, three in title III, and two in title IV) that had a statutory due date prior to February 2000. These six requirements are not included in figure 3.

Source: GAO's analysis of EPA's data.

It is important to recognize that in terms of their ultimate impact on the environment, all requirements are not equal. For example, a requirement that EPA issue a rule on monitoring a limited number of stationary sources in a single industry has neither the complexity nor the impact of a provision that requires dozens of states to submit implementation plans to attain a major national ambient air quality standard. The latter is inherently more difficult to accomplish and often requires states and local agencies to pass legislation and issue, adopt, and implement rules. Certain programs are implemented largely by states and require extensive, continuing interaction between EPA and the nation's governors, state legislators, county officials, state and local regulators, and others on numerous complex requirements. Other programs are implemented by EPA.

Overall, as of February 2000, EPA had fulfilled 409 of the 538 requirements that it identified to implement the amendments' first six titles. Of the 409 requirements that have been met, 247 had a statutory due date and 162 did not. The majority of actions required for five of the six titles have been completed. For example, EPA has completed 126 of 141 requirements implementing the NAAQS under title I.

The 129 remaining requirements include promulgating regulations for states and local air pollution control agencies to enforce, as well as other requirements described in the amendments. Of the 129 requirements that are unmet, 6 had a statutory due date prior to February 2000, 108 have a statutory due date after February 2000, and 15 do not have a statutory deadline. About one-half of these unmet requirements are for establishing standards for hazardous air pollutants: EPA is to promulgate 62 Maximum Achievable Control Technology (MACT) standards due by the statutory deadline of November 15, 2000.[7]

EPA missed the deadline for 198 of the 247 statutory requirements with a deadline through February 2000.[8] According to EPA officials, it is unlikely that the agency will meet the deadline for 62 of the 108 remaining statutory requirements. Specifically, the officials do not believe they will meet the November 15, 2000, deadline for establishing standards for hazardous air pollutants.

EPA officials cited several factors explaining why the agency has missed deadlines, including the following: (1) increased emphasis on stakeholders'

---

[7]These technology-based standards require the maximum degree of reduction in emissions that EPA determines achievable for new and existing sources, taking into consideration the cost of achieving such reduction, health and environmental impacts, and energy requirements.

[8]EPA has historically been tardy in meeting statutory deadlines. We previously recommended that EPA implement a rulemaking tracking system to aid the agency in meeting statutory deadlines, but EPA has not taken action on this recommendation. See *Clean Air Rulemaking: Tracking System Would Help Measure Progress of Streamlining Initiatives* (GAO/RCED-95-70, Mar. 2, 1995).

review and involvement during regulatory development, which added to the time needed to issue regulations; (2) the setting of priorities to manage the workload resulting from the 1990 amendments, which created a tremendous number of new responsibilities for EPA; (3) complications associated with the startup and effective implementation of new programs (e.g., operating permits and air toxics), which posed technical, policy, or legal issues that were not fully anticipated in 1990; (4) competing demands caused by the workload associated with EPA's response to lawsuits challenging some of its rules; and (5) the emergence of new scientific information and other factors that led to major Clean Air Act activities that did not arise from the 1990 amendments, such as the effort to reduce regional transport of ozone pollution throughout the East.

EPA officials stated that they do not believe they will meet the November 15, 2000, deadline for all of the remaining 62 MACT standards. (The agency took over 9 years to promulgate 92 existing MACT standards. According to EPA, these 92 MACT standards included some of the largest and most contentious categories.) The 1990 amendments require that if EPA fails to finalize the regulations within 18 months after the statutory deadline date, states must develop their own standards. According to EPA officials, this would be very expensive and cumbersome. However, the officials estimate that they can promulgate the required standards within 18 months after the deadline, noting that while the agency has missed previous MACT deadlines, it has virtually always issued the standards within 18 months of the deadline. According to EPA, in no case has any state had to develop its own case-by-case MACT determinations.

Views of Key Stakeholders on Major Issues Affecting Implementation of the Clean Air Act Amendments of 1990

The stakeholders we interviewed from environmental groups, industrial groups, and state and local governments stated that the Clean Air Act Amendments of 1990 have had positive effects on the environment by reducing pollutant emissions. However, the stakeholders had differing views on the issues that either helped or hindered the effective implementation of the specific provisions. Key stakeholders' views on the major issues affecting the implementation of each of the amendments' first six titles is detailed in appendixes I through VI.

The stakeholders we interviewed from environmental groups, industrial groups, and state and local governments identified three areas that affected the implementation of the specific provisions of the amendments: (1) the extent to which flexibility is allowed in meeting the requirements, (2) the specificity of requirements, and (3) the adequacy of funding at the state and local levels.

Extent of Flexibility in Meeting Requirements

One of the overarching issues affecting implementation cited by stakeholders is the tension between allowing states and sources of pollution the flexibility to develop their own approaches for achieving air quality improvements and using a more prescriptive "command and control" approach. For example, the title IV acid rain program, as designed by the Congress and implemented by EPA, attempted to strike a balance between traditional command and control principles—which specify where and how emissions reductions must be achieved—and the flexibility of market-based measures for reducing air pollution. Stakeholders from environmental and industrial groups and state and local governments told us that the flexibility provided by the acid rain program's sulfur dioxide emissions allowance-trading system enabled the required emissions reductions to be achieved at a lower cost than that estimated at the time the amendments were passed.[9] Other stakeholders pointed out that because the legislation specified the reduction goals and identified the power plants that were required to achieve these reductions, the program was administratively more efficient to implement.

According to some stakeholders, adopting more market-based approaches like the acid rain program is a particularly effective way of achieving greater flexibility. In their view, this program has shown that an aggregate "cap" on emissions, which permits individual sources to trade allowances, can lead to lower-cost emissions reductions than those under the traditional command and control approach used by EPA in other programs. EPA officials agreed that the "cap and trade" approach can lead to lower-cost emissions reductions (and, in some cases, reduced pollution levels as well) than those under a traditional command and control approach. However, they pointed out that to work effectively, cap and trade programs traditionally require a well-known population of sources with extremely well characterized emissions and control costs. According to EPA, other forms of economic incentive programs and approaches (e.g., open market trading and emission fee programs), in some circumstances, can be added to the existing regulatory structure and can provide incentives for

---

[9]Title IV of the amendments uses a market-based approach to allow electric utilities to trade SO2 allowances with other utilities. Utilities that reduce their emissions below the required level can sell their extra allowances to other utilities to help them meet their requirements.

reductions from other source categories when accountability is adequate. For this reason, EPA has issued rules and guidance that allow states and other stakeholders to consider a variety of economic incentive approaches to both reduce costs and gain improved environmental quality.

Concerned that future emissions reductions may be more expensive and difficult to accomplish, a state and local government organization official and other stakeholders cited a need for EPA and the states to provide flexibility in achieving further emissions reductions. According to one state official, allowing the states more creativity and flexibility is a way to get a better "bang for the buck" in emission reductions. He added that EPA should provide oversight but give the states the flexibility and incentive to meet the requirements themselves. We have reported several times in recent years on EPA's evolving efforts to provide states with more flexibility and to "reinvent" environmental regulation, under the Clean Air Act and other statutes, by incorporating more flexible approaches and a greater focus on environmental results.[10]

An industrial stakeholder observed that the Clean Air Act Amendments of 1990 allow EPA to use innovations such as trading mechanisms that would provide needed flexibility but that EPA had not used these innovations except in the acid rain program. However, EPA officials cited several examples that, in their view, illustrate the use of more flexible approaches.

---

[10]See *Environmental Protection: Challenges Facing EPA's Efforts to Reinvent Environmental Regulation* (GAO/RCED-97-155, July 2, 1997), *Environmental Protection: EPA's and States' Efforts to Focus State Enforcement Programs on Results* (GAO/RCED-98-113, May 27, 1998), and *Environmental Protection: Collaborative EPA-State Effort Needed to Improve New Performance Partnership System* (GAO/RCED-99-171, June 21, 1999).

- The Ozone Transport and Assessment Group—a national work group consisting of representatives of EPA, the Environmental Council of the States, and various industry and environmental groups—identified flexible and cost-effective strategies to address the long-range transport of ozone. These strategies, including emissions trading programs, were incorporated in the agency's 1998 rule requiring 22 states and the District of Columbia to revise their state implementation plans to mitigate the transport of ozone through a reduction in nitrogen oxides. The rule allows states flexibility to choose the best mix of controls to meet statewide emissions budgets.[11] EPA also published as guidance for states a "model rule" for achieving these emissions reductions through a cap-and-trade program.
- On the basis of the experience with the acid rain trading program, the Ozone Transport Commission developed a nitrogen oxides trading program for states in the Northeast, with EPA's assistance.
- In developing measures to be included in state implementation plans to improve visibility, EPA gave states the option of applying the best available retrofit technology on a source-by-source basis or developing an emissions trading program. EPA also cited the regional planning bodies that have been formed to address visibility impairment and regional haze issues as another example of flexibility.
- EPA's recent rule to reduce emissions from cars and light-duty trucks allows averaging, banking, and trading to provide additional flexibility to both vehicle manufacturers and gasoline refiners.

According to one stakeholder, the state implementation plan process—under which each state develops a plan for implementing, maintaining, and enforcing air quality standards—needs to be better coordinated and more flexible in order to address situations in which pollution from one state contributes to the air pollution problems in another.

EPA officials also noted that the agency worked with states and regions to design guidance on economic initiative programs that can be adopted to provide for the cost-effective implementation of the national ambient air quality standards. EPA believes that this guidance provides states with a great deal of flexibility in developing their implementation plans for achieving the air quality standards.

---

[11]63 Fed. Reg. 57, 356 (1998). This rule has been the subject of litigation. On March 3, 2000, a federal appeals court rejected most challenges to the rule, upholding EPA's authority to promulgate it. *Michigan v. EPA*, No. 98-1497 (D.C. Cir. Mar. 3, 2000).

Specificity of Requirements

Several stakeholders identified the specificity in the act or in implementing regulations as an important factor affecting implementation. According to an environmental group stakeholder, statutory provisions that specified the expected quantity of emissions reductions and identified the categories of sources that were expected to achieve the reductions have been more successfully implemented. For example, according to a state and local government organization, specifying the amount of sulfur dioxide emissions reductions to be achieved and the specific power plants where the reductions were to come from made it easier to achieve the required reductions in sulfur dioxide emissions. The stratospheric ozone provisions of title VI—which specify the affected chemicals and the time frames for the eventual phase-out of their use—were also cited by stakeholders as an example of successful implementation.

Adequacy of Funding

The states, state organizations, and environmental groups that we interviewed all commented that state and local governments need additional funding to more effectively implement the requirements of the act. According to a director of an organization that represents all state and local governments, there is currently a $140 million annual shortfall in funds at the state and local government levels.

EPA awards grants to the states and local government agencies to help them implement the Clean Air Act. The agency has reduced this funding over the last several years by 25 percent to $120 million annually. According to a state and local government organization, EPA justified the decrease by considering the funding available to states and local air pollution control agencies through permit fees (which are assessed on regulated sources for permits required by the Clean Air Act). However, according to a stakeholder representing an environmental group, there is a scarcity of funds from permits because states have been under pressure to keep the fees low. EPA officials stated that they work jointly with states and local agencies to establish priorities on the basis of available funding and, through work plan negotiations for grants, have been successful in directing grant funds toward agreed-upon priorities.

One state government stakeholder commented that much of the burden of implementing the Clean Air Act has now shifted from EPA to the states. For example, EPA provides grant funds for the purchase of equipment, but states are expected to provide a matching share of the money needed to operate it. Such a problem may surface in the case of the new monitors for particulate matter. EPA paid for the monitors, and, as we reported in 1999, is funding their operation and maintenance.[12] However, future funding for operation and maintenance was uncertain. According to EPA, the Clean Air Act recognizes that the states are principally responsible for its implementation, and through the appropriations of grant funds, the federal government participates in aiding the states in meeting their obligations.

Observations

The Clean Air Act is a large and complex statute. The nature of the pollutants covered by specific titles varies greatly in terms of, among other things, the distances they travel once airborne and how they interact with other pollutants in different climates and weather conditions. Moreover, the numbers of sources vary greatly depending upon the pollutant. One of the challenges facing the Congress in considering the Clean Air Act's reauthorization is determining the appropriate balance between traditional command and control approaches and more flexible approaches that allow state and local air pollution control agencies and other stakeholders to implement the most cost-effective strategies, while meeting national air quality goals. In this regard, the acid rain provisions in title IV could offer a worthwhile model for some other air quality problems by setting national emissions reduction goals and, at the same time, encouraging market-based approaches to achieve the national goals.

Agency Comments

We provided EPA with a draft of this report for review and comment. The agency stated that presenting a broad account of the status of its implementation of the Clean Air Act in a single report was difficult and offered several suggestions for framing the implementation status in a broader contextual perspective. We agree with the general thrust of these comments and have made changes to the report where appropriate.

---

[12]See *Air Pollution: EPA's Actions to Resolve Concerns With the Fine Particulate Monitoring Program* (GAO/RCED-99-215, Aug. 12, 1999).

Specifically, EPA emphasized that an assessment of the act should focus on results such as emissions reductions, air quality improvements, and the increased protection of public health and the environment and emphasized that these improvements can be achieved through cost-effective methods that allowed for economic growth. We added information in the report on emissions reductions, national air quality improvements, and the increased protection of public health and the environment. The agency also pointed out that the report focuses on the 1990 amendments' implementation without discussing related activities resulting from requirements established in prior clean air statutes, such as the requirement for periodic review and, if appropriate, revision to the national ambient air quality standards. Our objective was to review only the status of requirements added by the 1990 amendments. We made it clear that the report does not provide information on other requirements. EPA also stated that given the act's ambitious agenda and the reality of finite resources, the agency gave priority to implementing requirements that offered the greatest impact, which resulted in missed statutory deadlines for other requirements. We added this statement to the discussion of why EPA has missed deadlines. Lastly, we made changes to include EPA's views that the agency endeavored to implement the 1990 amendments in a flexible manner that best achieves air pollution reductions and that while the market-based cap and trade program has been highly effective in reducing sulfur dioxide emissions, it may not be the best tool for every environmental problem. The agency provided technical comments that updated and clarified information in the report; we incorporated these comments where appropriate. Appendix VIII contains the full text of the agency's written comments.

Scope and Methodology

To obtain information on the status of EPA's implementation of the Clean Air Act Amendments of 1990, we held discussions with the EPA officials who manage EPA's work load under the amendments' first six titles. As agreed with your staff, we did not review the status of implementing the 1990 amendments' remaining titles. We also did not address the status of implementing the requirements established prior to the Clean Air Act Amendments of 1990. We also obtained and reviewed EPA documentation entitled Implementation Strategy for the Clean Air Act Amendments of 1990. This document is updated periodically, provides an overview of the regulatory framework envisioned by the Clean Air Act Amendments of 1990, and provides information on what EPA has accomplished and what is left to be accomplished. We analyzed this documentation, including the most recent update in March 1999, and prepared a table of the requirements under each title, the requirements met by and after the established deadlines, and the unmet requirements. In order to ensure an accurate-as-possible count of the requirements, we asked EPA to review our table of requirements, and EPA suggested changes, which we have incorporated. For the requirements that were late in being met, we obtained agency officials' reasons for the delay. This analysis provides the extent to which EPA has met its requirements under the Clean Air Act Amendments of 1990 but does not show the extent to which the states and industry have actually implemented the requirements promulgated by EPA. We recognize that a tabulation of the requirements is only the first step in determining the status of implementation because of the relative complexities of the different provisions in the act. For example, certain titles require extensive, continuing interaction among EPA and state and local regulators, while others do not.

To obtain the views of key stakeholders on the major issues affecting the implementation of the Clean Air Act Amendments of 1990, we interviewed and received information from organizations that were interested and affected parties, including environmental groups, manufacturing associations, and state and local government agencies. (See app. VII for a listing of the organizations selected.) We coordinated our selection of organizations with EPA to ensure the representation of a good cross section of the key stakeholders involved with the implementation and oversight of the Clean Air Act Amendments of 1990. We asked representatives from these associations for their views on the implementation of the Clean Air Act Amendments of 1990, including factors that could either help or hinder effective implementation. We also obtained documentation of the National Governors Association's comments on the implementation of the Clean Air Act Amendments of 1990. We did not independently verify the information provided by the stakeholders. For each issue presented by the stakeholders, we asked for examples to support the points they were making. In some cases, examples were provided. We also asked EPA officials with responsibility for implementing the act to review and comment on the issues raised by the stakeholders.

We performed our work from May 1999 through February 2000 in accordance with generally accepted government auditing standards.

As arranged with your office, unless you announce its contents earlier, we plan no further distribution of this report until 30 days from the date of this letter. At that time, we will send copies of this report to the Honorable

Carol M. Browner, Administrator, Environmental Protection Agency, and other interested parties. We will make copies available to others on request.

If you have any questions about this report, please contact me at (202) 512-6111 or William F. McGee at (919) 899-3781. Key contributors to this report were Gregory P. Carroll; Hamilton C. Greene, Jr.; Karen Keegan; and Everett O. Pace.

Sincerely yours,

David G. Wood

David G. Wood
Associate Director,
    Environmental Protection Issues

Title I—National Ambient Air Quality Standards

The Clean Air Act authorizes the Environmental Protection Agency (EPA) to set national standards to protect human health and welfare from emissions that pollute ambient air. As a first step in this process, EPA is required to list harmful pollutants that are discharged in relatively large quantities by a variety of sources across broad regions of the country. The act requires EPA to determine National Ambient Air Quality Standards (NAAQS) for these so-called "criteria pollutants."[1] NAAQS are currently in place for six air pollutants: ozone, carbon monoxide, sulfur dioxide (SO_2), nitrogen dioxide, lead, and particulate matter. EPA has been regulating these criteria pollutants since the 1970 Clean Air Act amendments were enacted. However, title I of the 1990 amendments established a more comprehensive approach for states to implement, maintain, and enforce the NAAQS to further help reduce criteria pollutants.

Status of Requirements

To accomplish the objectives of title I of the Clean Air Act Amendments of 1990, EPA identified 141 requirements. These requirements included promulgating new regulations, such as enhanced monitoring for ozone, nitrogen dioxide, and volatile organic compounds; publishing final guidance for state plans to implement the NAAQS; and issuing reports to the Congress on volatile organic compounds emissions from the use of consumer and commercial products. The status of these requirements is shown in table 1.

---

[1]These pollutants are called *criteria pollutants* because the agency sets permissible levels for them on the basis of "criteria" or information on the effects on public health or welfare that may be expected from the presence of such pollutants.

Table 1: Status of Requirements Designed for National Ambient Air Quality Standards

Require Requirements with statutory deadlines	Number
Met on time	16
Met late	48
Unmet—deadlines prior to February 2000	1
Deadlines after February 2000	14
Subtotal	**79**
Requirements without statutory deadlines[a]	**62**
Total	**141**

[a]EPA has met all 62 requirements.

EPA's most recent data show that it has taken the required action to meet 64 of the 79 title I requirements established with a specific statutory deadline in the legislation. However, in 48 instances, the agency completed the required action after the statutory deadline had passed. According to EPA, it missed deadlines in the 1990 amendments owing in part to competing demands placed on the agency and other stakeholders by Clean Air Act issues not arising from the 1990 amendments. For example, in the development of new air quality standards for ozone and particulate matter, an extensive scientific consultation process occurred. The emergence of new scientific information documenting the importance of regional ozone transport led to EPA's extending the deadlines for state submittal of ozone plans for many areas, and engaged states and EPA in a 2-year process to conduct modeling studies and to study potential solutions. That process led to EPA's nitrogen oxides State Implementation Plan call, which was another major effort. In addition, many of the title I requirements were delayed because of litigation. EPA has recently been delayed in implementing recent revisions to the NAAQS for ozone and particulate matter and in implementing its plan to mitigate the interstate transport of ozone because of two recent court rulings in May 1999. As a result, several requirements planned for completion in 1999 and 2000 have been put on hold.

According to EPA officials, the ongoing litigation on particulate matter and ozone is the largest obstacle preventing EPA from successfully completing the requirements of title I of the 1990 amendments. EPA has implemented the bulk of title I requirements.

Views of Key Stakeholders on Major Issues Affecting Implementation of Title I of the Clean Air Act Amendments of 1990

The stakeholders we spoke with from environmental and industrial groups and state and local governments recognize the benefits of title I and acknowledge that cleaner air has resulted from it. As shown in table 2, the concentration of criteria pollutants affecting national air quality has decreased significantly from 1978 to 1997.

Table 2: Long-Term Percent Changes in National Air Quality Concentration

Numbers in percentages

Pollutant	Air quality concentration percent change, 1978-97
Carbon monoxide	-60
Lead	-97
Nitrogen dioxide	-25
Ozone	-30
Particular matter	Data not available
Sulfur dioxide	-55

Source: EPA's *National Air Quality and Emissions Trends Report* (1997).

However, stakeholders, including environmental groups and states, expressed concern with the process of implementing title I and gave several suggestions on how to improve the requirements or change the legislation. In particular, stakeholders support making improvements—such as better coordination between states and EPA and more flexibility–to the State Implementation Plan (SIP) process, which is required by all states to implement, maintain, and enforce the NAAQS. In addition, stakeholders expressed their concern with the inconsistency in the way that states implement NAAQS, which is generally allowed by the act, and suggested that the act provide for better coordination between EPA and the states to address these inconsistencies on a regional basis. Lastly, other stakeholders expressed their concerns with specific provisions in title I of the act that exempt older facilities from the emissions standards that apply to newer facilities.

State Implementation Plans Process

Several stakeholders, including the environmental and state groups we spoke with, support making changes to the SIP process required by all states when they implement the NAAQS. According to one stakeholder we met with, the SIP process needs to be coordinated better, more flexible, and based on performance. The stakeholder added that more flexibility was needed in the SIP process so that coordination between state and local entities and EPA can be more effective, especially when pollution from one state contributes to the air pollution problems in another. According to EPA officials, under section 126 of the Clean Air Act, any state may petition EPA to set emissions limits for specific sources of pollution in other states that significantly contribute to its air quality problem. Petitions were filed by eight states in 1997 and three additional states and the District of Columbia in 1999. In December 1999, EPA granted final approval of four of the eight petitions filed in 1997. By granting these four petitions, EPA found that certain large electric utilities and large industrial boilers and turbines violated a Clean Air Act prohibition against significantly contributing to air pollution in other states.

According to an independent research organization we met with, a late SIP puts a state transportation agency in a bind because EPA can automatically withhold federal funds. As a result, state planners must plan for two scenarios—one with federal funds and one without them. Using two scenarios results in additional planning time. According to EPA officials, the 1990 amendments to the Clean Air Act direct EPA to apply certain sanctions to areas that fail to comply with the act's requirements. These officials stated that one of these sanctions—the withholding of federal highway funds—takes effect only after a state or nonattainment area is 2 years late in submitting the required SIP revision. Before such sanctions are invoked, the Governor's office and other government officials are made aware of the pending action and also are advised of what must occur to remove the sanction.

According to the independent research organization we met with, a change to the current SIP process is supported. Under the change, credit will be given not only for planned programs, but also for going back and validating information through actual performance. For example, states are currently receiving SIP credits for instituting inspection and maintenance programs, but the credits are based solely on EPA's model—not on validating actual emissions testing. According to EPA officials, EPA does not discourage a state or area from validating its reduction credits. EPA reviews state validations by assessing the rate at which a state is reducing its total emissions.

Regional Solutions for Ozone

Several stakeholders expressed their concern with the inconsistency in states' approaches for implementing NAAQS, which are generally allowed by the Clean Air Act, and suggested that the act provide for better coordination between EPA and the states to address these inconsistencies on a regional basis. One stakeholder stated that the differences in states' approaches for implementing NAAQS need to be addressed, particularly in regions with ozone problems because ozone is a regional problem–not just a state problem. The stakeholder recommended that EPA be granted more authority to impose regional solutions to solve the interstate transport of ozone pollution. According to this stakeholder, one solution would be for the SIP process to be run on a regional basis. Another stakeholder suggested that in the area of ozone transport, there is a need for better coordination between states because none of them has the authority to require the others to take any particular action.

According to EPA, the agency has taken significant steps toward reducing ground-level ozone in the eastern half of the United States. Through a 2-year effort with the Ozone Transport Assessment Group, EPA worked in partnership with the 37 easternmost states and the District of Columbia, industry representatives, and environmental groups to address the regional transport of ozone. According to EPA, the process resulted in a comprehensive analysis of technical information related to ozone transport, including modeling and monitoring data. The Ozone Transport Assessment Group recommended flexible and cost-effective strategies for reducing the long-range transport of ozone and ozone precursors, including the development of trading and market-based incentives.

The solution to the ozone problem, however, has not been realized. In September 1998, EPA promulgated the nitrogen oxide State Implementation Plan call, a final rule requiring 22 states and the District of Columbia to mitigate the interstate transport of ozone through reductions in nitrogen oxides.[2] The final rule required the affected states to submit their State Implementation Plan revisions by September 1999, but on May 25, 1999, the U.S. Court of Appeals for the D.C. Circuit indefinitely stayed the deadline for submission of the required plans.[3] According to EPA, this court ruling delayed actions that would result in the reduction of actual nitrogen oxide emissions. On March 3, 2000, however, the federal appeals court rejected most challenges to the rule, upholding EPA's authority to promulgate it.[4] The court ruled, however, that EPA had improperly included 3 of the 22 states in the State Implementation Plan call.

In another ruling, the U.S. Court of Appeals, D.C. Circuit, remanded EPA's rules revising NAAQS for particulate matter and ozone.[5] EPA is seeking a review of the Court of Appeals decision in the Supreme Court.

Grandfather Clause for Old Power Plants

According to one environmental stakeholder, the most ineffective provision of the Clean Air Act is the grandfather language in section 111 (b)(6), which exempts coal-fired power plants existing at the time the act was amended in 1977 from the emissions standards that apply to newer facilities unless changes are made requiring permit modifications. According to this stakeholder, when this exemption—which covers most coal-fired power plants in the United States–was adopted, it was expected that these plants would be retired after approximately 30 years of operations and that the entire fleet of power plants would be replaced with lower-emitting, more-efficient facilities. According to this stakeholder, in practice, this provision has created an incentive for the owners of these older, dirtier power plants to continue to operate them long after their expected retirement dates and has slowed the development of cleaner replacement capability.

---

[2] 63 Fed. Reg. 57, 356 (1998).

[3] *Michigan v. EPA*, No. 98-1497 (D.C. Cir. May 25, 1999).

[4] *Michigan v. EPA*, No. 98-1497 (D.C. Cir. Mar. 3, 2000).

[5] *American Trucking Ass'ns. v. U.S. EPA*, No. 175 F. 3d 1027, *on rehearing* 195 F. 3d 4 (D.C. Cir. 1999).

This stakeholder added that the grandfather provision in title I imposes significant costs on society in terms of human health effects (e.g., medical costs for respiratory ailments and premature deaths) and environmental impacts (e.g., forest productivity losses, contaminated water bodies, and reduced visibility). According to this stakeholder, as the electric industry is deregulated, it is also increasingly clear that this provision has anticompetitive effects—making it difficult or impossible for new power plants to enter markets dominated by grandfathered plants, and consequently, limiting electric consumers' choice in the market. Any change in this provision would require a change in legislation.

In November 1999, the Department of Justice and EPA took enforcement actions against 32 coal-fired power plants, charging the companies with illegally releasing massive amounts of air pollutants for years. Because of the Clean Air Act grandfather provision, utility companies were not required to retrofit those existing plants with new air pollution equipment unless the utilities undertook major modifications of those plants. The government asserts that the utilities made major modifications to their plants in order to extend their life and to avoid the costs of building new plants, without installing new pollution control equipment, which resulted in tons of illegal emissions of pollutants. According to the EPA Administrator, the companies that owned the power plants had illegally retooled old, pollution-spewing coal plants without notifying regulators, without getting the necessary permits, and without installing new equipment to reduce emissions and meet pollution standards that apply to new plants. Most of these enforcement actions are still pending.

Titles I and II—Mobile Sources

Provisions for controlling air pollution from motor vehicles, engines, and their fuels are contained in both title I and title II of the Clean Air Act Amendments of 1990.[1] Mobile sources include cars, trucks, buses, trains, aircraft, motorcycles, construction and farm equipment, boats and marine vessels, and lawn and garden equipment. The Clean Air Act Amendments of 1990 provides for emissions reductions from transportation sources by emphasizing the following:

- *Title II, emission standards for motor vehicles:* Develop more stringent emissions standards for cars, buses, trucks, and nonroad vehicles and engines, such as construction equipment, boats, lawn and garden equipment, and locomotives.
- *Title II, clean fuels:* Develop reformulated gasoline, diesel fuel, and oxygenated fuels to reduce carbon monoxide emissions.
- *Titles I and II, inspection and maintenance and onboard diagnostics:* Develop programs to identify faulty emission controls and ensure that vehicles remain clean in actual customer use.
- *Title I, clean transportation alternatives:* Develop strategies to encourage transportation alternatives to address vehicle travel growth.

Status of Requirements

To accomplish the mobile source objectives of the Clean Air Act Amendments of 1990, EPA identified 89 requirements.[2] These requirements include promulgating new regulations to establish federal programs that resulted in cleaner passenger vehicles, trucks, and buses and cleaner-burning gasoline and diesel fuel. The amendments also authorized EPA for the first time to set national emissions standards for non road vehicles and engines, such as locomotives, boats, and marine vessels; lawn and garden equipment; and engines used in construction and agricultural equipment. The status of the implementation of these requirements is shown in table 3.

---

[1]In this report, we have included the discussion of major issues affecting the implementation of mobile sources programs from both title I and title II in this appendix. EPA's Office of Transportation and Air Quality and state and local air pollution control agencies operate their mobile source programs as one program.

[2]The number of requirements identified in this section relates to title II requirements only.

Table 3: Status of Requirements Designed for Mobile Sources

Requirements with statutory deadlines	Numbers
Met on time	6
Met late	21
Deadlines prior to February 2000	0
Deadlines after February 2000	0
Subtotal	**27**
Requirements without statutory deadlines[a]	**62**
Total	**89**

[a]EPA has met 51 of the 62 requirements.

EPA's most recent data show that it has taken the required action to meet all 27 of the mobile source requirements established by the legislation. However, as indicated in table 3, EPA was late in meeting 21 of its requirements. According to EPA officials, there were several reasons why the rules were late. One reason for the rules' lateness was that EPA began to operate differently in the early 1990s by bringing in more people to get their input and comments before issuing the rules. As a result, according to EPA, the process took longer but, in the end, turned out better because by the time the requirements were completed, most stakeholders were in agreement.

EPA officials believe that one of its greatest challenges will be to find ways to reduce emissions from motor vehicles, whose numbers and miles traveled continued to increase every year. According to EPA, despite the tremendous success of the federal program to reduce motor vehicle emissions over the past 25 years, they still represent the single largest category of air pollution in most cities around the country. An example of this challenge is the potential for an increase in the number of diesel-powered passenger vehicles that may enter the market in the coming years. The trend to more diesels is driven in part by their better fuel efficiency compared with gasoline engines. Diesels, however, produce significantly greater amounts of particular matter and nitrogen oxide than gasoline counterparts, according to EPA. Working with manufacturers of diesel engines to develop clean diesels for the future is one of the great challenges facing EPA in meeting the nation's clean air goals.

Views of Key Stakeholders on Major Issues Affecting Implementation of Titles I and II of the Clean Air Act Amendments of 1990

Several stakeholders from environmental and industrial groups agree that titles I and II of the 1990 amendments have made a significant impact on reducing pollution from mobile sources. For example, one environmental group stated that the emissions requirements for new vehicles have been quite effective in reducing emissions, as have the reformulated gasoline fuels programs. EPA estimates that oxygenated fuels reduced ambient carbon monoxide concentrations 7 to 14 percent overall for the winter seasons from 1986 to 1994. These groups, however, believe that improvements can and should be instituted in two areas involving mobile sources: (1) the inspection and maintenance programs and (2) considering and regulating pollution control devices and fuel requirements as one system.

Inspection and Maintenance Program

According to some state and local government stakeholders, and an independent research organization, although the inspection and maintenance program for in-use motor vehicles has resulted in significant reductions in emissions in the past, they are concerned that public support for the program may not remain. One state agency commented that improvements in the inspection and maintenance program, such as including the use of technology to lessen the program's costs, are needed if it is to continue receiving public support. In addition, the cost of the inspection and maintenance program has already led to declining support. Opposition to EPA's enhanced inspection and maintenance regulation—including the reluctance of some state legislatures to provide the legislative authority and funding needed to implement these programs—caused many states to delay implementation several years after the required start date of 1995.[3]

Opposition to what they view as the stringent requirements of the program led to the reluctance of some state legislatures to authorize and fund it. In order to decrease the cost, some stakeholders believe that there must be increased emphasis put on using new state-of-the-art technology, such as roadside testing using remote sensors, that is available to identify vehicles in need of repair. A stakeholder commented that these high-tech solutions to the identification of high-pollution-emitting vehicles are available but that they are not being used to the degree that they should. This

---

[3]See *Air Pollution: Delays in Motor Vehicle Inspection Programs Jeopardize Attainment of the Ozone Standard* (GAO/RCED-98-175, June 15, 1998).

stakeholder added that other types of in-use testing, such as remote-sensing devices, should be used instead of relying solely on inspection and maintenance facilities to identify vehicles needing repair. According to EPA officials, the agency currently allows states to use remote-sensing technology in their inspection and maintenance program as a form of "clean screening." These same officials said that a state might elect to use remote sensing to identify clean vehicles, whose owners would then be informed that it was unnecessary to bring their vehicles to an inspection and maintenance facility. In EPA's opinion, however, remote-sensing technology has not yet been demonstrated as a reliable alternative to replace standard inspection and maintenance testing. A stakeholder believes that the on-board diagnostic equipment, which is required in 1996 and newer model vehicles, should be used to identify problems in pollution-emitting vehicles instead of relying solely on inspection and maintenance equipment. According to EPA officials, on-board diagnostic equipment has been proven to be accurate in identifying high-emitting vehicles, on the basis of a recently completed 2-year test program. On-board diagnostic equipment has also been proven to reliably identify malfunctioning components and allow for more accurate diagnosis of vehicles' emission control systems than was possible with previous technology. EPA is currently working on a plan that will incorporate on-board diagnostic checks as part of state inspection and maintenance programs, and according to the agency, it will be implemented as soon as practical.

Vehicle Pollution Control Devices

According to one industrial stakeholder, the effectiveness of vehicle pollution control devices depends upon the types of fuels that are used in engines. The use of inferior fuels leads to less than desirable results in emissions reductions. Therefore, when one system is adopted without the other, opportunities for improving air quality are lost. The stakeholder is concerned that this interrelationship is sometimes overlooked. For example, according to this stakeholder, several northeastern states decided to require vehicles sold there to meet the pollution control requirements applicable to vehicles sold in California. The industrial group we interviewed commented that these states required California's vehicle standards but did not require California's fuels standards, and, thus, the effectiveness of the control devices was diminished. In addition, this group stated that the Clean Air Act should be changed to make it clear that advanced-technology vehicles like those required under the California standards should be used with cleaner-burning fuels like those required under the state's standards. EPA officials pointed out that in its recently announced vehicle program rulemaking, the agency, for the first time, considered vehicles and fuels as an integrated system and regulated each in a single rulemaking.

Title III—Hazardous Air Pollutants

Title III of the Clean Air Act Amendments of 1990 established a new regulatory program to reduce the emissions of hazardous air pollutants, specifying 189 air toxics whose emissions would be controlled under its provisions. The list includes organic and inorganic chemicals, compounds of various elements, and numerous other toxic substances that are frequently emitted to the air. Title III was intended to reduce the population's exposures to these pollutants, which can cause serious adverse health effects such as cancer and reproductive dysfunction.

Under the hazardous air pollutant program prior to title III, EPA identified only seven hazardous pollutants in 20 years and then developed emission standards for those pollutants using a risk-based approach. The approach of the new program differs from this in that, as a first step, title III identifies the pollutants to be regulated and directs that EPA impose technology-based standards, or Maximum Achievable Control Technology (MACT) standards, on industry to reduce emissions. As a second step, once EPA finishes the technology-based standards, it is to consider the remaining risks to the public and issue health-based standards to address such risk.

The act requires EPA to publish the technology-based emissions standards for both major and area sources from 1992 to 2000. The act also required EPA to publish a list of source categories by November 15, 1991, for these hazardous pollutants, but the agency did not do so until July 16, 1992. At that time, EPA listed 174 source categories. The Clean Air Act established milestones for issuing the MACT regulations as follows:

- ·Twenty-five percent of the MACTs to be issued by November 15, 1994.
- ·Fifty percent of the MACTs to be issued by November 15, 1997.
- ·One hundred percent of the MACTs to be issued by November 15, 2000.

Status of Requirements

To accomplish the objectives of title III of the 1990 Clean Air Act Amendments, EPA has identified 221 requirements. The implementation status of these requirements is shown in table 4.

Table 4: Status of Requirements Designed for Hazardous Air Pollutants

Requirements with statutory deadlines	Number
Met on time	15
Met late	102
Deadlines prior to February 2000	3
Deadlines after February 2000	94
Subtotal	**214**
Requirements without statutory deadlines[a]	**7**
Total	**221**

[a]EPA has met all seven requirements.

[b]The numbers in table 4 do not include the requirement for EPA to conduct residual risk determinations for each of the final MACT standards.

EPA's most recent data show that it has taken the required action to meet 117 of the title III requirements established by the legislation, although 102 of these were met late. As shown in table 4, EPA has 94 unmet requirements with statutory deadlines after February 2000. Ninety-two of the 94 requirements are to be addressed with the promulgation of 62 MACT standards. EPA took more than 9 years to promulgate the first 92 MACT standards. However, according to EPA, over that time period, it has taken much initiative in expediting the MACT development process. Nonetheless, EPA officials do not believe they will meet the November 15, 2000, deadline for all of the remaining MACT standards but estimate that they will do so for about three MACT standards. While they do not anticipate meeting the deadline for 59 MACT standards, they do believe they can promulgate the rules within 18 months after the deadline. This is significant in that the Clean Air Act requires that if EPA fails to finalize the rules within 18 months of the deadline, the states themselves must develop their own standards. According to EPA, this would be very expensive and cumbersome. EPA officials point out that while the agency has missed previous deadlines, it has virtually always issued the standards within 18 months of the deadline, and in no case has any state had to develop its own case-by-case MACT determinations.

According to EPA officials, the development of the MACT standards requires a significant amount of time and money. They explained that many previous requirements were met late because of the need to prioritize, given resource limitations, the time needed to develop the policy framework and infrastructure of the MACT program, and the complexity and stakeholder participation involved with some industrial source categories. EPA noted that the successful completion of the remaining MACT requirements is contingent upon adequate resources.

Views of Key Stakeholders on Major Issues Affecting Implementation of Title III of the Clean Air Act Amendments of 1990

Although EPA has not finished the technology-based standards, the stakeholders from an industrial group, environmental group, and state governments we interviewed stated that the program has been very effective, resulting in the reduction of millions of tons of air toxics and smog-forming volatile organic compounds from the air.

In the second step in the program to control hazardous air pollutants, EPA will assess the risk remaining to the public from these pollutants once the technology-based standards are in place. If necessary, the agency would then publish health-based standards to address that risk. It is in this second phase that some stakeholders from environmental and industrial groups, and state and local governments believe EPA will have the most difficulty. For example, one of the problems mentioned is that EPA will lack the necessary data to do the residual risks assessments.

Stakeholders are concerned that the second step–involving residual risk assessments– will be problematic. This second step will involve the evaluation of the risks remaining after the technology-based standards are in place and setting standards that are based on the risks to the public's health from air toxics remaining in the air. One industrial stakeholder commented that the "residual risk" program will be more difficult for EPA to implement, since it will involve defining what "risk" is, and "how clean is clean," as well as modeling issues. According to EPA officials, the agency is mandated to set a residual risk standard if the existing MACT standard does not protect the public health with an ample margin of safety. EPA outlined the general approach that it will use to make decisions whether to set residual risk standards in its peer-reviewed 1999 Report to Congress (EPA-453/R-99-001). The report states that, for carcinogens, EPA will continue to apply the 1989 Benzene National Emission Standard for Hazardous Air Pollutants, commonly referred to as the Benzene rule, which laid out EPA's approach for making decisions under the ample margin of safety language. Given that residual risk assessments will assess noncancer risks as well as cancer risks, EPA stated that it will use the best available models to assess residual risk and plans to apply them consistently.

In developing an overall approach to the residual risk program, EPA believes it may be able to learn from several states that have had risk-based programs. For example, over the last 15 years, Georgia has addressed residual risk by doing its own screening and modeling of the health effects of air toxics and set its own standards for allowable concentrations of toxins in the air. In addition, according to an industrial stakeholder, the upcoming residual risk program will require EPA to know a lot about individual industries and require an intensive data collection effort. According to EPA officials, they recognize that in many cases, conducting residual risk assessments will require the agency to expand upon the data collected for the development of the MACT standards. EPA states that it can gather these additional data from several sources, including EPA's National Toxics Inventory, state databases and permits, compliance reports, and industry. According to EPA, it will use the best available data to conduct residual risk assessment.

Insufficient data have caused data collection efforts in the past to be deemed unsuccessful. As a result, industrial stakeholders believe that problems with residual risk assessments will occur. According to one industrial stakeholder, because of time pressures and the lack of resources, EPA may be forced to make decisions using inadequate data. An environmental group stakeholder also commented that EPA would find it difficult to amass the information that will be necessary to develop the residual risk assessments. According to EPA officials, as with any risk assessment, there will be gaps in some data bases used and uncertainties in the results of the residual risk assessments. EPA stated that it would make every effort to collect the necessary data for these assessments and will clearly articulate the uncertainties that exist in the data as well as the assumptions used.

Title IV—Acid Deposition Control

Title IV of the Clean Air Act Amendments of 1990 establishes the acid deposition control program to reduce the adverse effects of acid rain deposition through reductions in the annual emissions of pollutants—mainly sulfur dioxide. It provides an alternative to traditional "command and control" regulatory approaches by using a market-based approach to allow electric utilities to trade SO2 allowances with other utilities to achieve cost-effective reductions. After setting the overall reductions in SO2 emissions to be achieved, the act defined each source's specific emissions limits and directed the allocation of allowances to sources in amounts equal to the emissions limits. These emissions limits for all sources are combined to meet a total emissions cap. The sources that emit SO2 must install continuous emissions monitors and keep records in accordance with regulations issued by EPA. The utilities that reduce their emissions below the required levels can sell their extra allowances to other utilities to help them meet their requirements. The utilities that exceed their emissions allowances forfeit allowances to cover the excess emissions and must pay fines that are set at several times the estimated average cost of complying with SO2 emissions limits.

In July 1997, we reported that the acid rain program, including the use of emissions trading, has been successful in achieving greater-than-planned reductions in the emissions of SO2 from facilities and projected significant cost savings compared with a traditional command-and-control regulatory approach.[1] More recently, we reported on trends in emissions and their effects.[2]

Status of Requirements

To accomplish the objectives of title IV of the 1990 Clean Air Act Amendments, EPA identified 44 requirements. These requirements included promulgating new regulations for an allowance-trading system, continuous emissions monitoring, and an acid rain permit program and issuing a report to the Congress on an acid deposition standard feasibility study. The status of these requirements is shown in table 5.

[1]See *Air Pollution: Overview and Issues on Emissions Allowance Trading Programs* (GAO/T-RCED-97-183, July 9, 1997).

[2]See *Acid Rain: Emission Trends and Effects in the Eastern United States* (GAO/RCED-00-47, Mar. 9, 2000).

Table 5: Status of Requirements Designed for Acid Rain Deposition

Requirements with statutory deadlines	Number
Met on time	9
Met late	15
Unmet—deadlines prior to February 2000	2
Deadlines after February 2000	0
Subtotal	**26**
Requirements without statutory deadlines[a]	**18**
Total	**44**

[a]EPA has met all of the 18 requirements.

EPA's most recent data show that it has met 24 of 26 of the title IV requirements established by legislation, although it was late in 15 instances. According to EPA officials, the agency was late with some of the requirements because interagency review and consultation with the Acid Rain Advisory Committee added time to the process. Officials consider that the time spent was worthwhile because it allowed for more stakeholders' input in the rules process, thereby making them less controversial.

According to officials of EPA's Office of Atmospheric Programs, Acid Rain Division, the program has been much more successful than initially envisioned—both in terms of emissions reductions and in terms of the cost to implement the program. Furthermore, they said the use of continuous emissions monitoring and the cap and trade program, which limits the amount of pollutants while allowing industry the flexibility to determine how best to reach those limits, can be considered as contributors to the overall success of the program. Also, EPA officials stated that both approaches might have applications to other pollutants and problems in addition to SO_2 for acid rain.

Views of Key Stakeholders on Major Issues Affecting Implementation of Title IV of the Clean Air Act Amendments of 1990

Stakeholders from both the industrial sector and from state governments whom we spoke with agree that, overall, title IV is one of the most effective titles of the Clean Air Act. Title IV serves as an example of a title that provides sources with the flexibility to reduce emissions cost-effectively—through the allowance-trading program—while establishing clearly defined objectives, firm deadlines, mandatory monitoring, and significant penalties for noncompliance. For example, one environmental stakeholder commented that the SO_2 emissions reduction-trading program has been implemented in a timely and efficient way and that emissions reductions are well documented as a result of acid rain reporting through the emission/allowance tracking system.

Currently, the control of nitrogen oxide under title IV does not include a cap on emissions nor provisions for nitrogen oxide trading. Stakeholders from an industrial group and a state would like to see the trading program's focus expanded, believing it could have beneficial applications to other pollutants associated with acid rain, such as nitrogen oxides, and also those not associated with acid rain. One of the stakeholders commented that if the trading program is employed for these pollutants, the program should provide the ability to trade emissions between sectors. For example, the mobile source component would be allowed to trade with the stationary source components. EPA agrees that a cap and trade approach could be applied to more air pollution problems and sectors, but emissions monitoring and accounting as well as administrative feasibility are important considerations in such expansion. EPA suggests that the approach should be extended to other stationary sources before considering its application to mobile sources.

Title V—Permit Program

The principal purpose of title V of the Clean Air Act Amendments of 1990 is to establish a national permit program to ensure compliance with all applicable regulations of the Clean Air Act. According to EPA, the program will enhance the agency's and the public's ability to enforce the act by making it easier to detect noncompliance and by requiring sources to take certain actions to demonstrate compliance. The program requires major stationary sources to obtain operating permits that contain all existing federal clean air requirements applicable to the source in one document. Title V was not intended to impose new substantive requirements. It requires industry to pay permit fees to cover the costs incurred by state air pollution control agencies in approving and administering these permits. According to EPA officials, over 18,000 sources have submitted permit applications. Of this number, approximately 7,000 permits have been issued.

EPA is responsible for promulgating regulations establishing the minimum elements of a title V permit program; reviewing, approving, and overseeing state programs; and reviewing permits issued by the states. EPA is also responsible for implementing permit programs for any states or tribal governments that do not implement their own programs. States are responsible for establishing and implementing their permit programs, issuing permits to pollution sources, collecting fees to cover the cost of the programs, and ensuring that sources comply with permit requirements.

Status of Requirements

To accomplish the objectives of title V of the 1990 Clean Air Act Amendments, EPA identified 14 requirements. These requirements included promulgating new regulations such as state permit program requirements, as well as publishing guidance on state programs to assist small businesses. The status of these requirements is shown in table 6.

Table 6: Status of Requirements Designed for the Permit Program

Requirements with statutory deadlines	Number
Met on time	1
Met late	2
Unmet—deadlines prior to February 2000	0
Deadlines after February 2000	0
Subtotal	**3**
Requirements without statutory deadlines[a]	**11**
Total	**14**

[a]EPA has met 8 of the 11 requirements.

EPA's most recent data show that it has taken the required action to meet the title V requirements established with specific statutory deadlines in the legislation, although EPA was late in meeting two requirements. For example, title V charged EPA, by November 1991, with issuing a permit rule that would identify the minimum elements of state permit programs and govern their implementation. According to EPA, disagreement between the Office of Management and Budget and the then Council on Competitiveness over certain requirements in the final rule delayed its issuance 8 months until July 1992. While waiting to learn what the final rule would require, EPA and the states postponed some efforts to implement title V.[1] In addition, after promulgation, states, industry, and environmental groups sued EPA over this rule, and EPA agreed to propose changes to portions of the rule to address litigants' concerns. According to EPA officials, the agency has moved the completion date for the rulemaking promulgating revisions to the operating permits program from April to November 2000 because of the need to repropose part of the package as a result of stakeholders' extensive comments. Until then, the original rule remains in effect, and states continue to issue title V permits.

---

[1]See *Air Pollution: Difficulties in Implementing a National Air Permit Program* (GAO/RCED-93-59, Feb. 23, 1993).

According to EPA's Office of Air Quality Planning and Standards, about 19,000 sources are subjected to the permit program. Between 18,000 and 18,400 sources had submitted permit applications. Of this number, 7,000 permits have been issued. As a result of the slow progress in approving permits, EPA has sought to identify and, where possible, correct the obstacles to faster permit issuance. The statute requires that permits be issued or denied within 3 years of the date that a state program is approved.[2] EPA officials predict an incremental climb in the number of permits being issued as a result of this effort. The effort has identified several reasons why the states have problems with meeting their established milestones. According to EPA, where possible, it has attempted to respond to these problems through guidance or other assistance. However, states also identified some internal issues. For example, one of the main reasons presented by the states is the turnover of permitting staff, compounded in some cases by hiring freezes and the lack of expertise that results when state staff leave and are not replaced.

Views of Key Stakeholders on Major Issues Affecting Implementation of Title V of the Clean Air Act Amendments of 1990

Some stakeholders from the industrial sector and from state governments questioned the cost-effectiveness of the permit program, observing that it does not directly lead to emission reductions, is more administrative in nature, and takes a lot of time and manpower. Industrial stakeholders also cited as an implementation issue the perceived inconsistency of EPA's interpretation of "modifications" to permits.

Cost-Effectiveness of Permit Program

According to EPA officials, Title V was added to address existing shortfalls in compliance. However, state agencies and an industrial stakeholder whom we interviewed agreed that the permit program consists primarily of accounting and reporting processes rather than inspection processes. One state stakeholder commented that the permit program attempts to enforce environmental rules through a paper trail rather than by inspections of specific sources. According to EPA, however, a permit that clearly contains

[2]Program approval dates range from December 1, 1994, to June 10, 1997.

all Clean Air Act requirements for a facility can serve as a valuable inspection tool.

A state stakeholder told us that title V is more administrative in nature than other provisions of the act, yet it takes more time and more manpower than anything the state must do under the Clean Air Act Amendments of 1990. From the state's perspective, the program has become an administrative grind: when the permits are finished, what remains is a voluminous document that few will read. According to EPA, the initial steps of getting the program up and running and issuing the initial round of permits certainly could require significant resources, but the act funds this effort with permit fees that sources pay to the states. EPA believes that since the permit is a single document containing all applicable requirements, it should be of interest and use to the industrial sources, air pollution control agencies, and the public.

When the permit program was implemented, several states already had permit programs in place. For example, according to a state official, California has had a permit program for 30 years and would rather enforce its regulations through inspections. According to a state stakeholder, the Clean Air Act Amendments allow for state permit programs that provide equivalent results, but EPA wants the permit programs in each state to be identical. According to EPA officials, the title V regulations allow significant flexibility in tailoring state programs, but each program must meet the minimum criteria established by the act.

Costs are associated with both approaches–paper trail or inspection–and several state stakeholders believe that the actual inspection of emissions is more effective than wading through volumes of permit paperwork. For example, according to an industrial stakeholder, one permit application for a source is 15,000-pages long and contains several thousand requirements. State officials commented that they would rather inspect the source than go through the voluminous permit package page-by-page.

However, according to EPA, preliminary data indicate that as sources undertake the compliance review required by title V, as many as 70 percent of them in some states are finding Clean Air Act requirements that they had been unaware of or had been complying with improperly. Actual inspections always have a place in an air program, according to EPA, and should continue. However, the process of compiling all requirements in a single place and the requirement that sources review and certify compliance with these requirements are clearly leading to the correction of instances of noncompliance that were not caught by inspection programs, according to EPA. This leads to actual emissions reductions and a more level playing field for sources, the agency said. According to EPA, it also complements the inspection approach by providing inspectors with a permit that clearly describes what requirements apply to the industrial source, thus enabling more efficient inspections.

From the industrial perspective, significant costs have resulted from the permit program with minimal, if any, air quality improvements. According to an industrial stakeholder, at the time of the permit program's enactment, EPA estimated that the program would have no costs. In 1992, when the first regulations were issued, EPA estimated that the permit program would cost $360 million. Industrial stakeholders said that the actual costs are substantial. According to the *First Annual Title V Report of the Clean Air Implementation Project*,[3] the cost of the permit program has averaged $100,000 per facility for the 20,000 facilities subject to title V, resulting in total costs of at least $2 billion just for the preparation of title V permit applications. For example, according to one industrial stakeholder, the automobile industry has spent millions of dollars in preparing voluminous permit applications, yet only two assembly facilities have received approved permits. According to EPA officials, early estimates of the costs of the program are uncertain and vary widely because of differing early interpretations of various requirements. For example, according to EPA, many industrial sources and states took a very strict view of the permit application requirements of EPA's rules, leading to early concerns about voluminous permit applications. According to EPA, when it learned of these concerns, it issued two guidance documents to clarify that applications need not contain such exhaustive detail.

EPA has since issued several guidance documents that clarify and streamline permit application requirements. For example, according to EPA, it worked extensively with stakeholders in the automobile manufacturing industry to develop streamlined monitoring reference materials for use in their operating permit. EPA's latest estimates are that the administrative burden of the permit program is about $10,000 per source per year, but it acknowledged that the total costs could exceed

---

[3]See *Getting the Title V Program on Track: Will EPA Make the Necessary Changes to It Policies? First Annual Report of the Clean Air Implementation Project* (Apr. 1999). The Clean Air Implementation Project is an organization of major industrial corporations, which joined together in 1991 to focus on a broad range of issues under the 1990 Clean Air Act Amendments.

$100,000 for some of the largest and most complex sources. EPA expects this burden to lessen after the initial round of permit issuance is completed.

By clarifying how Clean Air Act requirements apply to specific sources, and requiring responsible officials at the sources themselves to review their compliance with these requirements, EPA believes title V is achieving several direct and indirect air quality benefits. As the program is being implemented, EPA is compiling a list of benefits that sources, states, citizens, and EPA report finding. Such benefits to date have fallen into several categories: (1) emissions reductions as sources begin to comply with requirements they had previously not been complying with; (2) improving monitoring, which allows sources to ensure their compliance with the act and to discover and correct deviations from the act's requirements more promptly; (3) identification of, and subsequent clarifying and streamlining of, permit or rule requirements that were overlapping, unclear, or obsolete; (4) improvements in the development of rules benefiting the regulated community, as rule writers develop rules with an emphasis on how these rules will be implemented through permits; (5) an improved awareness of pollution control requirements, resulting in sources' improved ability to do comprehensive air quality management and for states to conduct regional air quality planning; and (6) improved public involvement in air pollution control decisions.

Permit Modification

A problem with the permit program, according to an industrial stakeholder we spoke to, is EPA's interpretation of section 502(b)(10) of the Clean Air Act. Under that section, permit programs must have provisions to allow changes within a permitted facility without a permit revision as long as (1) the changes are not "modifications" under any provision of title I, (2) the changes do not exceed emissions allowable under the permit, and (3) the permit holder notifies EPA and the permitting authority. The stakeholder stated that EPA has interpreted this section to mean that any change in a facility, regardless of how small, requires the permit's revision and the agency's permission. According to the First Annual Title V Report of the Clean Air Implementation Project, EPA's history of interpreting the term modifications shows how the agency significantly increased the level of review required for minor changes without revising its regulations. Under the current permit rule, whether a change constitutes a modification in large part determines whether an industrial source can change its manufacturing process without the necessity of a permit revision. The industry report found the following:

- Consistent with Congress's clear intention, the preamble to EPA's 1992 title V rule made it clear that minor changes do not constitute modifications.
- EPA subsequently announced, in numerous Federal Register notices, that states must treat minor changes as modifications.
- In an August 1994 proposal, EPA confirmed this revision of the original title V rule.
- In August 1995, EPA rescinded this interpretation and, consistent with its original title V preamble, announced that it would define "modifications" to exclude minor changes.

According to the industry report, EPA's history of changing its interpretation of modifications is an example of how title V should not be implemented, if the program is to meet the essential policy objectives.

According to EPA officials, the definition of "modification" has been difficult to interpret and remains the subject of litigation. However, according to EPA, this term relates to the system for revising permits and should not affect the initial issuance of permits. EPA expects to resolve the litigation before a significant number of permit revisions occurs.

A related issue concerns the timing of permit modifications. According to an industry stakeholder, under the Clean Air Act, sources are allowed to wait to make any changes in their permits until the permits are renewed, as long as the time remaining on the permits is 3 years or less. According to EPA officials, the 3-year time frame applies to newly promulgated requirements, but nothing in the act allows sources to wait for up to 3 years to incorporate requirements that they themselves trigger by making a change at a source.

Title VI—Stratospheric Ozone Protection

Title VI of the Clean Air Act Amendments of 1990 pertains to the protection of the stratospheric ozone layer. Such protection is to be accomplished by limiting the production and consumption of substances with ozone-depletion potential.

Title VI categorizes substances that deplete the stratospheric ozone layer as either class I (i.e., chloroflurocarbons, methylchloroform, carbon tetrachloride, and halons) or class II (i.e., hydochlroflourocarbons) substances. Title VI required the phasing out of the production of class I substances by January 1, 2000, except in the case of methyl chloroform, which is to be accomplished by January 1, 2002. Title VI also allows for an acceleration of the phaseout if Parties to the Montreal Protocol determine that the stratospheric ozone layer is depleting more rapidly then estimated earlier.[1] According to EPA officials, under the accelerated phase out approved by the Parties, class I production and import were phased out.

As for class II substances, the title provides, effective January 1, 2015, that it shall be unlawful to introduce them into interstate commerce or use except under certain circumstances. Such circumstances pertain to (1) substances that have been used, recovered, and recycled; (2) substances consumed in the production of other chemicals; and (3) substances used as a refrigerant in appliances manufactured prior to January 1, 2020. The production of class II substances shall be unlawful after 2030. According to EPA officials, the Montreal Protocol Parties accelerated the phaseout of class II substances as well, beginning in 2004.

Other sections of title VI concern the use, disposal, recovering, and recycling of class I substances during the service, repair, or disposal of appliances; industrial process refrigeration; and the servicing of motor vehicle air conditioners. For the class I and class II substances being phased out, title VI provides for approving the replacement of chemicals, product substitutes, or alternative manufacturing processes that will reduce the overall risks to human health and the environment.

Status of Requirements

To accomplish the objectives of title VI of the 1990 Clean Air Act Amendments, EPA identified 29 requirements. These requirements

---

[1]On September 16, 1987, twenty-four nations signed the Montreal Protocol on Substances That Deplete the Ozone Layer, which called for specific reductions of chloroflurocarbons and halons.

included promulgating class I phaseout regulations, new class I labeling regulations, bans on nonessential products using ozone-depleting substances, and determinations of acceptability for alternatives to class I and class II substances and issuing reports to the Congress on the production/consumption of ozone-depleting chemicals. The status of the implementation of these requirements is shown in table 7.

Table 7: Status of Requirements Designed for Stratospheric Ozone Protection

Requirements with statutory deadlines	Number
Met on time	2
Met late	10
Unmet—deadlines prior to February 2000	0
Deadlines after February 2000	0
Subtotal	12
Requirements without statutory deadlines[a]	17
Total	29

[a]EPA has met 16 of the 17 requirements.

EPA's most recent data show that it has taken the required action to meet all 12 deadlines of the title VI requirements established by the legislation. EPA met all the deadlines, although, as indicated in table 7, it was late in meeting 10 of its requirements. For example, the Clean Air Act Amendments of 1990 required EPA to promulgate the mobile air-conditioning recycling regulations by November 1991; however, EPA did not meet this date. The regulation was promulgated in July 1992. According to EPA officials, the basic reason for being late with the requirements was the need to prioritize the large workload under the act.

Views of Key Stakeholders on Major Issues Affecting Implementation of Title VI of the Clean Air Act Amendments of 1990

The stakeholders we interviewed from both the industrial sector and the environmental sector agreed that title VI has been effective in reducing ozone-depleting chemicals from the environment. According to two industrial stakeholders, the most effective requirements under title VI are (1) the recycling and emissions reduction program for class I and II substances and (2) the servicing of the motor vehicle air conditioners rule.

According to one stakeholder, EPA faces a challenge to implement the regulations judiciously so that ozone-depleting pollutants can be removed from the ambient air in a timely manner. According to EPA, the basic reason why regulations are issued late is the lack of sufficient EPA staff to handle the large work load. Delays in issuing regulations may result in the emission of ozone-depleting substances or their substitutes into the ambient air. For example, absent a final rule addressing the recovery of refrigerant substitutes, some industrial refrigeration owners or operators may be venting refrigerant, while others may be complying with the statutory requirements of the Clean Air Act. The latter are likely following the detailed requirements set out in an EPA proposal that regulates the recovery of substitute refrigerants.

Selected Organizations Included in GAO's Review

Organization	Purpose
Air Conditioning Refrigeration Institute	The national trade association representing manufacturers of more than 90 percent of U.S.- produced central air-conditioning and commercial refrigeration equipment.
Alliance of Automobile Manufacturers	A coalition of nine global automakers that provides member companies a forum to work together on public policy matters of common interest and to work with government and other stakeholders to find sensible and effective solutions to improve the environment and motor vehicle safety.
Alliance for Responsible Atmospheric Policy	A coalition of companies that produce and use chlorofluorocarbons, hydrochlorofluorocarbons, and hydroflourocarbons. Coordinates industry's participation in the development of international and U.S. government policies regarding ozone protection and global climate change.
American Lung Association	A health organization formed to fight lung disease and promote lung health through education, research, and advocacy.
American Petroleum Institute	The primary trade association for the U.S. petroleum and allied industries engaged in oil and natural gas exploration, production, transportation, refining, and marketing.
Association of International Auto Manufacturers	The trade association for U.S. subsidiaries of international automobile companies. The association acts as the voice of the International Automakers in America, speaking to the public, the press, and the government.
Chemical Manufacturing Association	Represents the chemical industry on public policy issues, coordinates the industry's research and testing programs, and administers the industry's environmental, health, and safety performance improvement initiative.
Clean Air Network	An alliance of nearly 1,000 national, regional, state, and local citizens groups that work to protect human health and environmental quality.

Continued

Edison Electric Institute	The trade association of shareholder-owned electric utilities, whose members generate and distribute more than three-quarters of the nation's electricity. The institute provides information on energy and environmental issues of national importance.
Natural Resources Defense Council	Actively involved in major national environmental issues and many regional and international issues as well. Its primary strategies include scientific research, public education, lobbying, and litigation.
Resources for the Future	Nonprofit and nonpartisan think tank that conducts independent research—rooted primarily in economics and other social sciences—on environmental and natural resource issues.
State and Territorial Air Pollution Program Administrators/Association of Local Air Pollution Control Officials	Association representing air pollution control agencies in 54 states and territories and over 150 major metropolitan areas. The association serves to encourage the exchange of information among air pollution control officials; enhance communication and cooperation among federal, state, and local regulatory agencies; and promote good management of our air resources.

Continued from Previous Page

We also interviewed representatives from four states—California, Georgia, Illinois, and New York—and the nation's largest local program—California's South Coast Air Quality Management District. The state and local programs were chosen in coordination with EPA and the State and Territorial Air Pollution Program Administrators/Association of Local Air Pollution Control Officials to select a nationwide representation of the organizations responsible for implementing the requirements of the Clean Air Act Amendments of 1990.

Comments From the Environmental Protection Agency

UNITED STATES ENVIRONMENTAL PROTECTION AGENCY
WASHINGTON, D.C. 20460

MAR 2 9 2000

OFFICE OF
AIR AND RADIATION

Mr. Peter F. Guerrero
Director, Environmental Protection Issues
United States General Accounting Office
Washington, DC 20548

Dear Mr. Guerrero:

Thank you for the opportunity to review your draft report entitled "Environmental Protection Agency: Clean Air Act's Implementation Status and Issues." We appreciate the difficulty of providing a broad account of the status of Clean Air Act (CAA) implementation in a single report. As the report acknowledges, the agenda set out in the CAA is virtually unprecedented in its scope and has diverse elements that involve multiple levels of government and reflect strategies tailored to different types of air pollution problems. An assessment of the effectiveness of the CAA should focus on results -- emissions reductions, air quality improvements, and protection afforded to public health and the environment. An accounting of regulations issued and deadlines met is an additional element, but should not be the primary consideration. A review of the results achieved shows that the CAA's implementation has been highly successful. By working cooperatively with our state and local partners, citizen groups and the regulated community, we, together, have significantly improved air quality in the United States through cost-effective methods. Our experience shows that cleaner air and economic growth can go hand in hand.

Progress in Cleaning the Air

To appreciate how far we have come in reducing air pollution, it is instructive to remember where we were before the 1990 amendments. There was growing concern about the increasing damage to the stratospheric ozone layer, which, among other things, protects us from skin cancer and cataracts. Acid rain essentially was unchecked, causing damage to aquatic life, forests, buildings and monuments, as well as visibility degradation and health risks from sulfate and nitrate particles. Photochemical smog, which can impair lung function, cause chest pain and cough, and worsen respiratory diseases and asthma, exceeded healthy levels in 98 metropolitan areas in 1990. Many cities did not meet the national air quality standards for the pollutant carbon monoxide, which can aggravate angina (heart pain), and also for particulate matter, which is linked to premature death, aggravation of pre-existing respiratory ailments, and reductions in lung capacity. The millions of tons of hazardous air

-1-

Printed on Recycled Paper

pollutants emitted annually in the United States were largely unregulated at the federal level. Many of these pollutants have the potential to cause cancer or other serious health effects such as nervous system damage, miscarriages or birth defects.

The CAA Amendments of 1990 passed Congress with overwhelming and bipartisan support. Since then, the CAA has enabled this nation to substantially reduce each of the major air pollution problems that faced the United States:

·   Sulfur dioxide emissions, a primary precursor of acid rain, have been cut by more than 5 million tons from the 1980 level, and rainfall in the eastern U.S. is as much as 25 percent less acidic.

·   The U.S. and other developed countries have ceased production of the most harmful ozone-depleting chemicals and -- provided the U.S. and the world community maintain the commitment to planned protection efforts -- the stratospheric ozone layer is projected to recover by the mid 21st century.

·   Ground-level ozone pollution, particulate matter, and carbon monoxide pollution have all been reduced significantly, producing dramatic decreases since 1991 in the number of areas in "nonattainment." Between 1990 and 1997, total annual emissions of "criteria" pollutants (those governed by air quality standards) dropped by 10 million tons.

·   Cleaner motor vehicles and fuels are one important reason for these air quality improvements. New cars, trucks, buses are far cleaner than in 1990 as a result of EPA emissions standards. Thirty percent of the gasoline consumed in the U.S. is cleaner-burning reformulated gasoline, which reduces emissions of smog-forming VOCs and toxics. Substantial reductions are being achieved for the first time through standards for non-road engines in locomotives, bulldozers, marine vessels and lawn and garden equipment.

·   Rules issued since 1990 are expected to reduce toxic emissions from industry by 1.5 million tons a year -- eight times the reductions in industrial toxics achieved in the previous 20 years.

It is important to note that these improvements have occurred simultaneously with strong economic growth and increased productivity. EPA has sought to implement the CAA efficiently and effectively through a combination of rules, voluntary measures, market mechanisms, state partnerships, and stakeholder negotiations. The progress reflects cost-effective implementation of the CAA, as well as improvements in the efficiency of industrial technologies.

-2-

Although EPA and its state and local partners have completed much of the specific work laid out in the 1990 amendments, a great deal must still be done for the nation to achieve clean air. As GAO notes, more than 100 million Americans live in counties where the air does not meet the national air quality standards. Ground-level ozone pollution and fine particle pollution continue to pose health threats in many areas of the country, and we still have major challenges ahead to reduce regional pollution transport. Continued efforts to reduce toxic air emissions, acid rain, and threats to the stratospheric ozone layer are needed if the Clean Air Act's goals are to be achieved. One example of the work ahead is EPA's ongoing effort to propose new, more stringent exhaust standards for large diesel trucks and buses, along with requirements for cleaner diesel fuel. Although EPA has already put in place the specific standards required by the 1990 amendments, many areas of the country need additional emissions reductions from this large source of nitrogen oxides (NOx) and particulate matter.

The Report's Scope and Focus

GAO may wish to note that because its focus is the 1990 amendments, the report does not discuss all CAA implementation activities resulting from requirements established prior to 1990, or from scientific advances during the past decade. Some of these activities have affected implementation of the 1990 amendments. For example, the CAA mandates periodic review and, if appropriate, revision of national ambient air quality standards. The draft report does not discuss EPA activities to build the infrastructure for implementation of the ozone and particulate matter standards revised in 1997, or the impact of ongoing litigation on implementation of those standards. Also, a scientific consensus developed over the past decade regarding the regional nature of the ground-level ozone problem in this country and the need for substantial reductions in nitrogen oxide emissions. This eventually led EPA to issue a rule calling for regional NOx controls in the East (the "NOx SIP call"), one of the most significant CAA regulatory initiatives of the decade.

The report seems to emphasize the counting of met and unmet statutory requirements. This could lead to serious problems if the figures were used as a basis for comparing EPA's success in implementing one title of the Amendments with another. If such comparisons are included in this report, they should recognize the differences in challenges presented by different pollution problems and different programs. For example, certain programs are implemented largely by states and require extensive, continuing interaction between EPA and the nation's governors, State legislators, mayors, county officials, State and local regulators, and others on numerous complex requirements. Some programs involve especially difficult technical, policy or legal issues. Such differences must be considered in any evaluation of EPA's success in implementing the CAA.

-3-

EPA suggests that the draft report's discussion of views on the Title V operating permits program, to achieve better balance, should more fully describe benefits of that program. We will provide you with additional information on this point.

Statutory Deadlines

GAO correctly notes that EPA has completed most of the rules and other activities required by the CAA through the present. GAO also observes that many requirements were completed after the statutory deadline.

In assessing this record, EPA believes it is important to consider the environmental results mentioned above. We would also elaborate on the reasons that deadlines were missed:

·	The 1990 amendments set tight deadlines for an unprecedented number of new actions by EPA, including development of major new programs (e.g., air toxics, acid rain, operating permits) and emissions standards that involved controversial, precedent-setting and complex issues important from environmental and economic standpoints. At the outset, EPA recognized that extensive involvement of state and local leaders, industry and environmental groups would be necessary if the CAA was to be successfully implemented. This collaborative approach added to the time needed to complete many rulemakings. In a number of cases, EPA conducted formal or informal regulatory negotiations with all the stakeholders prior to proposing regulations. These historic negotiations were successful in reaching agreement on several very complex programs, such as the reformulated gasoline program. The time spent in these up-front discussions, although often lengthy, paid off by getting stakeholder agreement early in the rulemaking process.

·	The array of deadlines in the 1990 amendments required EPA to move forward simultaneously with states and stakeholders on multiple major rulemakings, placing multiple demands upon EPA managers and key non-EPA participants. Some programs (e.g., air toxics) involved multiple, interrelated rulemakings that were moving ahead simultaneously, and changes in one ongoing rulemaking could affect another, causing delays.

·	Some deadlines were missed because the programs required by the 1990 amendments involved very complex, technical, policy and legal issues that were likely not fully understood by Congress when it established the deadlines in 1990. These issues took significant time to solve. Examples are the requirements in Title 2 that EPA establish emission standards for numerous categories of non-road engines. None of these categories (which include locomotives, construction and farm equipment, boats and lawn and garden equipment) had ever been regulated by EPA for air emissions. Thus, EPA had to identify and meet many times with industrial companies that had no prior experience in designing or manufacturing their products to meet low emission levels. Often, new technologies or variations on existing technologies had to be developed to be compatible with the specific operating characteristics

-4-

of these non-road engines. All of this took time and, for good reason, often meant that EPA missed the established deadlines.

· Major competing demands were placed on EPA, states and stakeholders by CAA issues not arising from the 1990 amendments, including scientific and other issues. One example was the development of the new air quality standards for ozone and particulate matter, including an extensive scientific consultation process. In addition, EPA undertook an extensive stakeholder consultation process on implementation issues. Another was the emergence of new scientific information documenting the importance of regional ozone transport. This led EPA to extend deadlines for state submittal of ozone plans for many areas, and engaged states and EPA in a two-year process to conduct modeling studies and to study potential solutions. That process led to EPA's NOx SIP call rule, another major effort. The workload entailed with response to litigation on some rules also caused competing demands.

· Some implementation activities are more important than others because they have greater impact (e.g., the NOx SIP call). The ambitious agenda in the CAA, given the reality of finite resources, inevitably required EPA to stage the timing of implementation activities to ensure that the most important activities were given priority, which resulted in missed deadlines for other activities. EPA would suggest that the draft report places disproportionate emphasis on resources relative to other reasons for missed deadlines.

CAA Implementation Statistics

At GAO's request, EPA has reviewed the counts of CAA amendment requirements developed by GAO. GAO with EPA assistance has endeavored to make these requirement counts as exact as possible given time constraints.

GAO's "Observation" Regarding Trading

EPA agrees that the acid rain program has been highly effective as well as less costly than predicted, and that its market-based cap-and-trade SO2 allowance system is a model that should be used to address additional problems when appropriate. EPA already has been working with states to apply this model to another regional air pollution problem -- NOx emissions which contribute to interstate transport of ozone pollution. The Ozone Transport Commission with EPA assistance developed a NOx budget and trading program for states in the Northeast, and the OTC and EPA are jointly implementing the trading system through an innovative partnership. Building on this effort, EPA issued a model cap-and-trade rule as guidance to assist states in implementing the NOx SIP call, which sets state NOx budgets over a broader area of the East. The experience of the acid rain program shows that this approach has potential to achieve regional reductions in an efficient and highly cost-effective manner.

-5-

We would add that trading is not the best tool for every environmental problem. In weighing the application of trading, among factors to consider are the technical and economic feasibility of monitoring or estimating emissions with sufficient accuracy to provide accountability, the significance of localized health or environmental impacts of emissions, the feasibility of obtaining agreement on emissions baselines for establishing a trading program, the viability of the emissions market for the universe of sources in question, and the administrative feasibility of allocating and tracking emission allowances or credits. States and EPA have a broad menu of regulatory and non-regulatory tools, each with strengths and weaknesses. For each environmental problem, a choice among these strategies should be made based on the particular circumstances of that problem.

Implementation Flexibility

EPA has endeavored to implement the 1990 amendments in a manner that provides flexibility on ways to achieve the necessary air pollution reductions, with accountability for the results. An excellent example (though by no means the only way we have promoted flexibility) is our expanded use of emissions averaging and trading. Tested in the 1980s, emissions averaging and trading today are standard tools of the air program. Beyond the NOx and acid rain programs mentioned above, EPA has used trading to provide flexibility in the phase-out of CFCs and in many national rules to reduce emissions from vehicles, engines and fuels. One recent example is the recently finalized Tier II/gasoline sulfur rule to reduce emissions from cars and light-duty trucks, which allows averaging, banking, and trading to provide additional flexibility to both vehicle manufacturers and gasoline refiners. We also have provided compliance flexibility through averaging and/or other means in numerous air toxics emissions standards.

Because states have primary responsibility for implementation plans to achieve national air quality standards, EPA has assisted states in establishing trading and other economic incentive programs, such as California's RECLAIM program for reducing sulfur dioxide and nitrogen oxide emissions and the OTC NOx program mentioned above. EPA also has issued guidance to allow states to count voluntary measures to reduce emissions from transportation sources -- such as ridesharing programs and ozone action days -- toward their state planning requirements under the Act.

Detailed comments on the draft report are included in an enclosure. Thank you again for the opportunity to comment.

Sincerely,

Robert D. Brenner (for)

Robert Perciasepe
Assistant Administrator

Enclosure

-6-

Ordering Information

The first copy of each GAO report is free. Additional copies of reports are $2 each. A check or money order should be made out to the Superintendent of Documents. VISA and MasterCard credit cards are accepted, also.

Orders for 100 or more copies to be mailed to a single address are discounted 25 percent.

Orders by mail:
U.S. General Accounting Office
P.O. Box 37050
Washington, DC 20013

Orders by visiting:
Room 1100
700 4th St. NW (corner of 4th and G Sts. NW)
U.S. General Accounting Office
Washington, DC

Orders by phone:
(202) 512-6000
fax: (202) 512-6061
TDD (202) 512-2537

Each day, GAO issues a list of newly available reports and testimony. To receive facsimile copies of the daily list or any list from the past 30 days, please call (202) 512-6000 using a touchtone phone. A recorded menu will provide information on how to obtain these lists.

Orders by Internet:
For information on how to access GAO reports on the Internet, send an e-mail message with "info" in the body to:

info@www.gao.gov

or visit GAO's World Wide Web home page at:

http://www.gao.gov

To Report Fraud, Waste, or Abuse in Federal Programs

Contact one:

- Web site: http://www.gao.gov/fraudnet/fraudnet.htm
- e-mail: fraudnet@gao.gov
- 1-800-424-5454 (automated answering system)

PRINTED ON RECYCLED PAPER

United States
General Accounting Office
Washington, D.C. 20548-0001

Official Business
Penalty for Private Use $300

Address Correction Requested